# A BIRD BETWEEN

## Spencer M. Carney

v1.0

NOTION

an imprint of Wordwraith Books

# A BIRD BETWEEN
## by Spencer M Carney

Printed in the United States of America
First Printing, 2017
ISBN 978-1-946921-93-2

Notion
An imprint of Wordwraith Books, LLC

705-B SE Melody Lane #147
Lee's Summit, MO 64063

e-mail *wordwraiths@gmail.com*
website *www.wordwraiths.com*
Twitter *@Wordwraiths*

Edited by Kallie Falandays
Cover Design by Austin Helling
Format Design by Rod A. Galindo
Spencer's website *spencermcarney.com*
*Spencer's Twitter @spencermcarney*

For Linda Brock who assigned extra credit,
and for Kristin, who inspired this incarnation of
my art to evolve

# Foreword

Day and night can be quite blurred
Within the city that is always heard

Twenty-four hour lights
And underground tunnels
Can keep the stars out of sights
Your focus spinning in funnels

From the youth going out to party
Or the waiter staying up late
To the downtrodden begging for money
And the zealot in the subway spouting hate

Yet if you listen closely at any hour
The lyrical sounds of morning are consistently sung
By avian artists that carry sun and moon on each
  wing
Outside of time they live eternally young

With feet in parallel worlds
Living on the borders between spaces
Singing an aria of tranquility
They mock closed minds with harsh faces

Over trees of every origin
Through bars of construction or windows of
  shattered glass

A Bird Between

Above skyscrapers and between beams
    of light that pierce the stratosphere
The mockingbird melody binds it all

## A Show-Me State

At what point does a vine pull away from a fence

Letting its guard down, dropping every defense?

That magical moment

When its leafy hand

Departs for the unknown

Ready to make a stand


Only sunlight beckons it on

It reaches out for divinity

No longer a barbed fence

This vine seeks infinity


Through with reaching links in a chain

A desire to curl and twist in the air

Intuition the only guide

The vine jumps into the glare

But though this vine is quite splay

It rears its head in light of day

## Crystal Skies Over The Fields

My father loved rainstorms

We would watch them together on the porch

Like this one

                    simmering over the fields of wheat

Bit by bit bullets pelt the earth

After its many complaints for drink

Together we'd marvel at the dramatic spectacle

He'd point out the meteorological instruments at

  play

Show me how what was once retaliation

Becomes a rock concert only heaven could produce


After the final song

Electric guitars of thunder and lightning

## A Bird Between

Melt

                        into singular tears falling on piano keys

Sunlight drips through the clouds


Absolute stillness falls

When I look at the sky

                                            as I do now

I see him

                                    his face in awe

Savoring the rapture before the clouds bid adieu

As must we all

## The edge of the forest bordering the farm

The songbird sings a tune aloft in a tree

I whistle back with years of admiration

The birds of my youth my first friends

A sudden smile tugging at my lips as his head jerks

  in bewilderment

A riff

    a tweet

        a rising aria

Becomes the exchange of two strangers speaking

  different languages

His frustration at not being understood takes him

  to another branch

Then another

        higher up he goes

He spreads his wings and takes flight off into the

  distance

Towards the ghost-bird he longed to understand

I look deep into the direction he flew

An un-explainable thread drawing my heart

  forward

His talon

        the other end

# Crossing State Lines

I rumble along the gravel to the cement highway

# A Bird Between

The road stretched out before me like the canopy

  of a dogwood

Seizing my chance to fly away

Focused on my impending adulthood

Traffic exits reveal new pathways off in different

  directions

Buildings like so many leaves at the end of each

  branch

I wrap my mind around the possibility of so many

  connections

To a space so new and different from back home

  on the ranch

Rolling down my window I feel the wind in my hair

I breathe in the fresh air and my new-found

  freedom

Finally, I feel that I can lay my soul bare

All it takes now is knowing that I can beat'em

All roots are attached to the same soil

I brim with confidence that my plans will not foil

# Driving across the country

The stars are above

Holding promises and the dreams

Of those who flock to the big white letters on the

   hill

Pockets of

                                   City lights twinkle below

Their golden light

Paling

In comparison to the suns above

Warm in my car

                                                   I can

Sit back as I cruise down the road

The expanse of space

                                   spread out before me

The country is all around me in this in-between

   place

Traveling from here to there

Passing pockets of power plants

                                   collections of buildings

Piercing the dark

                              with their rounded golden glow

Wondering

Wondering if the light is bright enough to contain
  me

The only one on the road

I slow down

                                        to a stop

I look up at the many eyes shining in the night

They watch me with intensity

Some say the stars can foretell your fate


## Arriving In The City of Angels

Warm California sun kisses my skin for the first
  time.

Soft gossamer flowers gently fall from the trees.

Calm and serene is the rush of water in nearby
  pools.

The wind softly brushes my face,

and barely graces the leaves of the trees with its
  presence.
Just as the struggle of winter is a myth in this place,
So the rush of new life that comes in spring.
Fall comes for vacation, but finds no chilly friend.
I pick up the idea of, "Hawaiian time", though on
  the mainland.
Feelings of unlimited time fill me as my life spreads
  out before me.
Oh! What a paradise you'll find!
In the land of eternal summer.

# Mini Mid-City Circus

A single

                                        small spider

A veritable sky dancer
Liltingly holding fast to its strand of near-
  transparent salvation
A backdrop of graffiti
painted into a circus of colorful characters

## A Bird Between

The fall to the spectacle floor

                                                    Is long

Jagged sidewalk uprooted by a coast live oak

But spiders are known to fly

With their strand holding only the open sky

The spider's silent

                                    focused in their art

as there is no spider song

Only the wind gently rustling leaves

Though the spider jostles along her phantom

   ribbon

Taking her life into her many hands

She sets her eyes on her dream

All that awaits

                                    A Leafy menagerie


# Waiting for the bus on San Vicente

A lethargy overcomes me as I sit in the sun

Its golden glow washes over my body

Lest fragments of shade allow it to be shun

The warmth I feel being absorbed into my skin

The light seeping into my soul

Tiny perspiration: a sign that Helios will win

Not Phelgon or Pyrois, nor Aethon or Aeos, a foul

For a brief moment all of Gaia, the great earth,
　goes dark

As clouds float by, a cool breeze rushes past

My skin jumps at the stark

Time slows down for a moment

Just when the sun returns, so too, the feelings of
　somnia

Actively waiting for my chariot must suffer another
　postponement

As my eyes give into another round of lethargia


## Overcast At Santa Monica

I see the eye of the world

Where Western Sea meets Western Sky

Many a man who looked too deeply there have
　died

# A Bird Between

But here I am safe on a soft beach

Dozens of children playing, and parents easing

  within the ocean's lull

Shrieks of laughter and frivolity

Muffled by the undulation of the waves

The worries of the city drowned out

Like a distant echo softened in caves

This eye is only visible when there is no SoCal sun

Frigid air bites shrewdly

Yet the young still have fun

As a void, the eye of the world seems daunting

Many who stare into it feel lost

The price of aging, comes, at a cost

Yet I know a secret, explorers of yore did, too

Sailing into the eye by starlight

Will eventually yield a clue

The eye becomes a horizon

Bringing new daylight to come

Wisdom that should be known to many

But is only known to some

# The Hummingbird Quarter On Campus

Life is aflutter with the simmering sonata of
   summer
The perfume of the leopard lily wafts through the
   air as sensuously as the spindly curvature of the
   stems
 They hold the floral heads, ever-unwieldy
light dances with the fragility of wings that reflect
   like a lense-flair
Splaying an equally ethereal display of shadow to
flint across the aged bricks that pave the court
the foliage blushes fuchsia and lavender atop a
backdrop of ever-green and vibrant lime
One hummingbird sits tenuously on a high perch
scanning the area for his next flute of nectar
At first his earthy color catches the sunlight  finding
   a back of azure
Then quiet settles over the patio, turned glade

As the hummingbird rests his bejeweled eyes on

some oddity

A gust of wind

a drop of a petal

a blink

The hummingbird has vanished

A fading reverb of faerie music left in its wake

## Lime Tree at The Sublet Off Hauser

There is a lime tree in my backyard

Heavy with acidic fruit

Far in the back alongside the garage

There this lime tree blooms

Perhaps it might be nice to linger there

And rest in the hammock beneath the tree

If only the dogs didn't poo around it

The smell at war with your nose

It's nice to know it's there though

Like some opportunity waiting to be had

If only we had such a thing as winter

Covered with snow it might be nice

Limes themselves protect their inner purity

Only their rind can be tainted and rough

Living in the city can be hard

But within we all have a lot to offer

## Heaven Laid Bare in Burbank

In the garden of the church

I watch as clouds billow in, expectant with rain

On marble bench I make my perch

Witness to a heavenly stain

The day is still warm, though zephyrs blow

I clutch my book determinant

Armed against the windy flow

Struck by the celestial firmament

# A Bird Between

When a cacophony of cathedral bells rings around

I peel away from the welkin

Yet I gravitate to those painters who don't make a

   sound

Accompanied with the light of my fallen kin


The heavens twist in a meteorological blessing

As artful and as temporary as life's stages

I feel separation, the organ inside begins playing

Pressing the image into my mind's pages


## A fountain within a college campus

I look at my reflection

                                 at the edge of the basin I see

an ever-flowing fountain

My inherent structure

constant

brings tranquility

But my surface is effervescent with crystal droplets

   dancing

change

Physically

                                    a fountain

With mild wear and tear from acid rain

pigeon droppings

still holding strong to my molding

But my inside

The liquid of my life...?

I extend my hand to the water


# Griffith's Racket Shroud

The sound of nature is smothered

Even here

                                    It's not the same

Bursting car horns, blasted music, booming air
   travel

If it were quiet, you'd hear quite a different riot

The breeze lightly rustling the silver appendages

 that bend just across my vision

The chatter of squirrels

The gentle cooing of mourning doves unseen

The delicate snap of a leaf breaking from its branch

The crunch as the leaf is welcomed by the grass

And maybe

> just maybe

The yearning for the living tree it left behind

Grass

> or Tree

Tree

> or Grass


## The Local Outdoor Community Recreation Center

The little soldier ant braves the perils of a jungle made of grass. To him, each blade must be the size of a redwood. Bent on his mission, he is completely oblivious to the giant human sitting cross-legged observing him. Unlike the human giant, a fallen soldier ant would not have a nuclear family who would grieve his demise. Do hive minds notice when one of their scouts goes missing?

In his wake, the soldier ant leaves scent trails marking where he has gone. Continuously, soldier after soldier will follow the trail to its end. Only to meet the same fate as those left behind, even if that fate meant falling into obscurity. Suddenly, with one thunderous step, the giant human is miles away from where the ant stood. Neither the worse for the wear that a being of greater power had just determined his fate.

# Potted Plant At The Bougie Hog

I'm just here to look pretty
To not get in the way
To add a bit of color
An accent to your day

My name is Fred
Yes I have a name

Chosen they said

Hollywood is for fame

My desire is to be truly noticed

Not to just be ignored

The greenhouse was the remotest

Here I could be adored


All around me a theatre

Here in this little café

Conversations to savor

As humans go and stay


But you push me aside

More room for your plates

Deep within I learn to hide

My confidence deflates


## Collection of Mushrooms Alongside Exposition Blvd.

More and more I feel myself,

Slipping,

Slipping into my imagination.

Ascending police siren.

I turn to look.

My shoe.

Trips me up.

A rusty manhole cover.

Ow...

Oh!

Mushroom caps.

Platforms.

No, Parasols!

For the faeries.

An alien encampment.

See the saucer-like spaceships?

Atop curvy towers.

I'm small.

Like Alice.

No!

Thumbelina?

Fungle Jungle. Danger.

Suspense.

In and out.

                                Weaving throughout.

Cap to cap.

I jump.

                                The nearest stem's back.

Shimmy down.

BOOM!        BOOM!        BOOM!

A lady.

                                Gathering recyclables.

Returns to her shopping cart.

                                Lifted eyebrows.

Giggling.


## Friend in Nature: Somewhere in Culver City

Alone in my home

I feel my heart slowly sink

Waiting for the sun to rise

The promise of connecting with another

A branch enters through the window and says hello

Lush flowers extended

A fragrant magnolia champaca

Swiftly soothes my heart

Here in my home

I find that a friend has found me

Grew just outside my window

The entryway barely open

I caress the soft petals

While I lean on the sill

Reminded of a different time


## An Attempt at House Plants

Today's the day it was decided

In the sink we will drink our fill

A sterilized basin with repellant chrome


Side by side we tuck in our crusty leaves

Our roots mashed to our plastic bottoms

We pray and hope that he notices

There is only so much nutrients in this soil

When you can't breathe it doesn't matter

How prickly or colorful or sturdy you are


We wait and wait for a human to come

There isn't a choice when you aren't connected

Earth beneath you and sky above


Two days later he makes an appearance

Apologizes and fusses with the faucet

Water running on us like aluminum paper


Our time has past

Unable to be quenched

Wishing for music that never came


## A Thicket in Your Eye


Can we know the depths of another's soul?
The demons and angels that make someone
    whole?

Searching, shifting, slipping along...
Are they a monster, has something gone wrong?

Are actions enough to pave the way,
such as someone giving or deciding to stay?

Gaze into their eyes when you shout hello or
　whisper goodbyes
When you make a joke or hypothesize.

The eyes of a dog never lie
Everything for them is at the surface.
But humans are quite different, you see.
With many layers and years that alter purpose.

Many try to live their lives openly
The secrets they keep even unknown to
　themselves.
'Til the day comes when the unexpected shows up
Knocking the mind's shelves.

At times, this can be a blessing,
A spring cleaning, or a catharsis.
Other times, it might feel a curse.

Knowing the name of your demon
Is only part of the game.
Vanquishing him? Just the same.

For the human mind is a tangled web,
A moonlit forest,

Beautiful works of art, but
Remember, it's hard to know every part.

## Waiting for the Subway

Deep in the caves
Like so many bats
We wait for the snake
Keep eyes out for rats

They sense it will come
The wind blowing fast
They bundle their wings
The time to wait past

The tunnel lights up
And all the bats stir
Snake eyes will flash gold
Be quick to check fur

The serpent is here
All flutter in teeth
It slithers away
Like a cunning thief

In the snake's belly
I find my seat
Careful to move
I watch my feet

With a small twitch
Made a wrong move
Bat screeches loud
I must improve

# Downtown

Columns of cement and iron fill

This valley with small boxes that explode red and

  green

Overhead then shut in a flash


The granite floor gritty and unmoving I hear

noise within the labyrinth aloud with the screams

  of those

unhinged accompanied by screeching of rubber on

  pavement


In the background of grey the clatter of nameless

Faces who scurry independent of one another each

  makers of these strange edifices

A Bird Between

Expanse of blacktop creates a wind

Tunnel only heard below the rumbling clamor

Traffic creates speeding down the intersections

The silence filled with scurrying roaches

Worried slowing down would bring sudden

Doom under the feet of the faces and the crushing

   sound-bytes

## Mindscape

I dance around

                    my mindscape

Vast wilderness

             stretching out before me

Just

              A snap of my fingers

Deciduous limbs

                      One

With the open sky

I leap about

                    within my escape

Rivers and meadows

                    crop with each step

Waving clouds along

                    with a playful swipe

I survey

                    the landscape

My palm

                    dusts off a mountainside

Finds refined steel

                    interlaid copper wire

low humming

                    I rip my hand back

Look up

                    singed palm

Barren waste

                    power lines

I pull tighter

                    at my cape

## A Bird Between

Rippling

                              flapping in the wind

I soar

                              further into the abyss

# The Letter Left Behind in Apartment 214

To my landlord,

I had dreams of visiting a metropolis

Where life burst forth from every rafter

Yet I only mourn for coming generations

Who will never know nature's song


I know you won't grieve me

That another will take my place

Your life will continue as it had

My time is up, it won't be long


My heart still burns with hope

That soon mankind will understand

Though every day the silva

Awaits the final gong

# Lovers at Hermosa

A blanket of glass washes up on shore
rolls back into folds of crystalline liquidity
the sand rendered a marble surface
slick enough for sea nymphs to skate across.

The ocean sings on a breath
that starts with a hiss and ends on a crush.

Sailboats gently glide along the surface
smooth, sloping, serene

White light collects around the vessels' surfaces.
The gold splashed across the oceanic canvas
As if an angel bumped a pale of celestial light.

As the wind picks up,
the waves grow larger;
mist sprays off the silver peaks
like steam on metal being forged

the sand,
in its great affection for the sea,
mirrors its tumultuous lover
as grains pick up into the wind

as both dance in the breeze
dusk melts into frame.

The land receiving the ocean more
with each throe of passion.

Under the soft aurora of moonlight
the embrace of mist and sand deepens.

## Moving On: The Open Skies Above Southern California

The sky is clear
No cloud in sight
I spread my wings
Jump to take flight

Up there so blue
Not much to see
It feels so slow
The endless to be

Down below
A canvas so lush
I reach the ocean
my view flush

Azure above
Deep brackish below
Two sides of a coin
Oh where to go

Night falls slowly
The sun sets low
The sky lights up
The stars are aglow

The heavens burn bright
A kingdom to explore
Endless stars alight
New world to adore

# Memory: Union with Nature on Midwestern Lake

On a speedboat

Green water mists my face

The sun is at its highest point

refracting crystalline drops in the whooshing water

I'm able to reach down

                        touch the mercurial liquid

My fingers split its form into wings

# A Bird Between

As small as a dragonfly

                              with a touch of grace

As large as a heron

                         with a dunk of my hand

A glass glove

                                        drips

down my arm

as I return to the craft

An aurora of light

                                  twinkles

when I turn my hand


I hold the sun

# ABOUT THE AUTHOR

**Spencer M Carney** is a Poet, Actor, and Musician that currently resides in Los Angeles County. Raised in the KC metro area, Spencer can say he is a native Missourian. Ever since he can remember, he has been enchanted with Nature's beauty. He is forever grateful to his parents for instilling that gift. Spencer studied English Literature and Composition for about two years at the University of Missouri-Columbia; before graduating with his Bachelors in Theatre from the University of Southern California. No longer a "Closet Poet", Spencer is hopeful this won't be the last you hear of him!

For more about Spencer M Carney, to follow his writing and other artistic pursuits, follow him on Twitter or Instagram… @spencermcarney
Or check out his website…
www.spencermcarney.com